AMANDA LATRICE

STRATEGIC STEWARDSHIP
Workbook

Strategic Stewardship Budgeting Workbook

Amanda Latrice, MBA

Strategic Stewardship Budgeting Workbook

"***Strategic Stewardship Budgeting Workbook***" *is designed to equip households with understanding of their finances and how to strategically begin to budget and analyze from a place of governing their households to align with the kingdom vision and mandate for their families.*

euodooenterprises12@gmail.com

euodooenterprisesllc.com

Connect with Amanda Latrice via Facebook or YouTube

Copyright 2018 – Euodoo Enterprises, LLC. All rights reserved.

Images are either copyright free, public domain images or used with permission of the graphic artist.

This book is protected by the copyright laws of the United States of America. This book may not be reprinted for commercial gain or profit. The use of occasional page copying for personal or group study is permitted and encouraged. Permission will be granted with written request.

Amanda Latrice, Visionary

Amanda Latrice is the founder and visionary of Euodoo Enterprises which was launched in August 2015. In December of 2008 she became burdened by lack of understanding surrounding finances and business strategy that was happening in the body of Christ and wanted to educate individuals, business, and communities on how to effectively budget, govern, and understand their finances and the internal structures of business.

Amanda is a strategist in the spirit and is an upcoming leader in her generation in the area of business. She graduated from Ball State University in 2010 with a Bachelor's Degree in Accounting and a minor in American Sign Language. In August of 2015 she graduated from Indiana Wesleyan University with a Master's in Business Administration and a concentration in applied management. She has been working and volunteering in Human Resources, Administration, and Accounting since she was in high school and has become trained in system integrations, implementations, policy and procedures, and internal structural development in each position she has carried.

She is a member of Kingdom Shifters Christian Empowerment Center in Muncie, IN where she serves as an administrator, an elder in training, and member of the intercessory team. She is also the administrator of Kingdom Wellness Counseling and Mentoring Center, and Kingdom Shifters Ministries, where she brings strategy and structure with a kingdom mindset accompanied with a business perspective. She has helped to establish dance ministries, orchestrate conferences and ministry events, and has traveled in ministry consistently, while ministering in the areas of dance, prayer, spiritual warfare, and deliverance. Amanda has a prophetic mantle which encompasses a strong deliverance and healing anointing. Additionally, Amanda possess the gift of administration, dance, teaching, and all manner of prayer. She also carries the mantle of wealth which drives her passion to see the Kingdom of God impact the market place. Amanda has such a heart and a passion to see individuals, kingdom businesses, communities, and ministries succeed and take on a business mindset with a kingdom perspective that will impact their communities and generations to come.

Table of Contents

Financial Governance 1
Who I Am in Christ Jesus 7
Strategic Sowing 11
The Beauty of Consistency 13
The Beauty of Consistency Prayer 15
Sowing and Reaping 16
Month 1 21
Month 2 37
Month 3 53
Month 4 70
   Household Budgeting Declaration 71
Month 5 88
Month 6 105
Month 7 122
Month 8 139
   Regional Authority Declaration 140
Month 9 156
Month 10 173
Month 11 190
Month 12 207
   New Business Owner's Declaration 208
   Year End Reflection 225
   Sowing in the Press 226
   Financial Prayer 228

Financial Governance

*What does it mean to govern and align your
household with the kingdom of God?*

Governing our households positions us specifically to direct, guide, influence, and regulate. We essentially are the gate keepers of our households and we determine what stays in and what must come out. We determine the rules and jurisdictions that operate within our household. In the natural, governing authorities have laws, rules, and regulations that help them guide and regulate their region or sphere of influence. Their job is to exercise or enforce the functions and systems of that government. The same applies in the spiritual realm. The kingdom of God has specific spiritual laws. As governors and kingdom heirs we will enforce the standards and laws of the kingdom in our households. We will direct our household spiritually and naturally in a way that completely aligns it with the truth and provisions that God has specifically for us.

<u>Govern is defined as(dictionary.com,2018):</u>
1. to rule over by right of authority
2. to exercise a directing or restraining influence over; guide
3. to hold in check; control
4. to serve as or constitute a law for
5. *Grammar.* to be regularly accompanied by or require the use of (a particular form).
6. to regulate the speed of (an engine) with a governor
7. to exercise the function of government
8. to have predominating influence

<u>Align is defined as(dictionary.com,2018):</u>
1. to arrange in a straight line; adjust according to a line.
2. to bring into a line or alignment
3. to bring into cooperation or agreement with a particular group, party, cause, etc.
4. to adjust(two or more components of an electronic circuit) to improve the response over frequency band, as to align tuned circuits of radio receiver for proper tracking throughout its frequency range, or television receiver for appropriate wide-band responses
5. to fall or come into line; be in line
6. to join with others in a cause

One of the definitions for align refers to a frequency for a TV or a radio station. In order to hear or receive from those particular channels the receiver has to be in tune with the correct frequency. The same applies to us as kingdom heirs. In order to truly receive the strategy and blueprint that God has for us personally and as a household we have to be in tune with him and properly positioned to be able to hear him clearly for what his instruction are concerning our household. The Kingdom of God is under the rule and dominion of the King of Kings. We are considered kingdom heirs as his children. Our true identities and destinies were birthed forth from the very essence of king himself, and because we are kingdom heirs and we birth forth from this kingdom all rights and privileges of the kingdom of God have been conferred upon us. Learning the kingdom rights and privileges that we have as kingdom heirs is a pivotal mindset shift. It allows us to recognize that we have the right to ask the father for his strategy and blueprint for our households and that it is his good pleasure to do so.

It sounds really poetic and beautiful to say align and be in tune with the Holy Spirit in order to receive instructions for your household and be able to govern it. Although this is true I am sure there are some that still are saying, "exactly how do you do that again?" I am so glad you asked! There is not one sure fire way that God will speak or give us instructions, so we do have to remain open to him. However, below are some suggestions as to how to govern and align your household with the kingdom of God so that more defined instruction can be released to us:

1. Find scriptures that will build you and your family up as kingdom heirs and decreeing them out loud.

    a. Finding scriptures allows you see what God has already said about you and your household and the access he gave you simply because you are his. Decreeing them out establishes them and also builds the truth up in you so that as situations arise, or counterfeit blessings arise you know the difference and are confident in what God has already said. Part of governing is knowing what rights and access we have as kingdom heirs. When we are unaware of who we really are, we do not fully operate within our reach and sphere of influence or we give our access/keys to the enemy to operate within our households, generations, and regions thus giving him permission to place constrictions where God has said we have limitless access.

2. Repent, Cleanse, and Heal from wounds that hinder full prosperity from operating in your life.

    a. As you are decreeing out what God has said for you and your family take time to repent for anyway you have mishandled the areas you are decreeing out. Our finances are tied to the prosperity of our soul (*3 John 1:2*), and often times, the mishandling of finances is not just an equipping issue, there is something in our soul where we have been wounded, hurt, disappointed, or simply wanting love and acceptance and our finances can manifest those wounds, hurts, and insecurities. For example, I had a client who felt like they just did not make enough money to handle everything. I had them complete an exercise where for two weeks they listed everything that they spent money on. After the time was up I sat down with them and they could clearly see where they were spending excess money. When I first looked at the spending patterns, and I could see they had a splurge that was just for them, but it was an outrageous amount. I asked my client did they feel like they never get anything for themselves and when they do they have to give it up. Their immediate answer was absolutely yes! For this client they felt devalued and it manifested in their finances by outrageous splurges. Take time to repent and ask God to heal areas of hurt or frustration in you where it is manifesting in your finances or any area of your life where prosperity is not operating in its fullness. Cleanse from shame and guilt and shut any doors that have been opened personally, generationally, or regionally.

3. Take time to journal what God is saying to you during your prayer time. It may not seem like it is tied to your finances but keep in mind that our finances are tied to the prosperity of our souls. We may find in our time of journaling that it is a place to release but also a place where God himself can release to us as well. This would be a place where the definition of the blueprint that God has for us and our household can be released.

4. Break the cycles, renounce them, fall out of Agreement with them, and do it differently then you have done it before.

    a. To get something different we have to do something different. We have to acknowledge there are ways in which we do things that are not getting us the results we desire. Ask God to show you what cycles and behavior patterns you operate in and begin breaking the cycles by renouncing and coming out of agreement with them, but also shift into handling occurrences and situations differently. Ask God to point out to you when you are operating from a cycle and then ask him to teach you what to do instead. Ask right in that moment as well as in your prayer time so that you are truly receiving the training that you need to truly align.

    b. Some examples of cycles in finances could be:
        i. Emotional spending such as shopping therapy-Those moments where you feel stressed or as if nothing is just for yourself; one may become impulsive and overspend buying really expensive gifts to treat themselves. Although there is nothing wrong with treating yourself make sure that it is not from an over emotional place. Spending from that place causes one to spend even when they do not have the funds because they are trying to fill a void, but they have opened the door to lack and an increase in debt. To break this cycle, you must choose to give up the right to fill our own hurts and frustrations. Take time with God and repent for every place that you have tried to take control. Break any vow that you have made about your finances and "YOU" making sure you are taking care of "me and mines" instead of allowing God to be the provider. Begin to declare out your healing and ask God to show you and deal with the root of why you emotionally spend. When that emotional impulse to purchase starts to happen DO NOT give in. In that moment ask the Lord to show you how to processes where that desire is coming from and how to deal with it. Recognize the truth of that moment and know that this desire is the enemy's subtle way of attempting to snatch your inheritance and chose to stay with God as he processes you to healing and wholeness.

ii. Obligation Giving- Constantly feeling like it is your personal obligation to take care of loved ones financially. We are always taught to take care of our loved ones no matter what, and to not do so is dishonoring. However, we are strategic sowers and as much as we may love them we can not heal the places in them that keep them from financial wealth. It is not our job to fill any void as the only one who can do that is God. We also need to be aware that we may be breaking generational (naturally and spiritually) curses of poverty and lack and we cannot break what we are feeding so we have to be willing to break ties of false obligation and allow God to heal any places in us and in our generational lines that go against what he is saying for our lives. Ask the Lord to reveal seasons where this shows up to shift your focus or drain your finances to where you cannot do as you planned. I am not saying we cannot give to our loved ones, but we have to be strategic in asking God when and how to so that he is honored in what we have sown.

iii. Giving for love, acceptance, and affection- giving to others based off your own personal need and void that needs to be filled. Attempting to buy love, time, and affection by purchasing gifts for those we desire to be around. This steams from rejection. Begin to break all ties with rejection. Break any way you have been accepting and become accommodating to the spirit of rejection. Break any way you try to keep control of the narrative and the dynamics of relationships so that you do not get hurt. Break all falsehood of true relationships and what love is. Ask the Lord to teach you about the Love of the father and to heal every place that you have used your finances to gain love, acceptance, or affection. Begin to ask God for the value that he has for you and break anything that is resistant to that. Also ask the Lord to show you the root of your rejection and also the seasons that it constantly shows up in your life. Allow him to deal with that area to bring healing, deliverance, wellness, and truth. Begin to embrace the value and truth of who God says you are and how important you are to him. Begin to do scripture affirmations to get in your spirit that will build up your view of who you are and your trust in God as your father. He knows your heart and will not withhold any good thing from you. He will provide the people in your life that will accept and love you and give balanced affection. Trust that he loves you and you are not forgotten by him. Allow him to heal you so that when those relationships come you recognize them and can receive them.

5. Cleanse from fear of lack and anyway fear has given you a by "any means necessary" mentality.

   a. Tenacity is a good attribute to have. It gives us a relentless focus and a drive not to give up even when its hard and trust what God is saying concerning our financial well-being. However, it is our actual focus that can turn tenacity into an impure object of affection that can hinder the fullness of prosperity from operating in our lives. In the corporate world we are taught to step on the backs of others to make sure we have the money we desire or need. The impure focus allows the door to greed to open and the love of money to become the root of evil. Ask God to remove anything in your heart that would cause your financial focus to be one of greed or the "by any means necessary mentality." Repent for anyway the mentality has caused you to step out of the character of God to control or speed up the process. Ask the Lord to heal any areas that have been wounded from others stepping on you to get what they want and any way you have tried to protect yourself and in turn you lost the true focus and integrity of God concerning your finances.

1 Timothy 6:10(ESV)
For the love of money is a root of all kinds of evils. It is through this craving that some have wandered away from the faith and pierced themselves with many pangs.

To be clear, MONEY IS NOT EVIL, it is the love of money that is the root of all kinds of evils. It is the impure focus on money that causes money to be the root to evil. Money has a proper place in our lives and when our focus is on money only it allows it to become our god instead of the true and living God. When we open ourselves up to greed we open ourselves up to the "by any means necessary" mentality which will allow us to step on others to get to where we want to go or where our focus resides. The scripture warns us that God does not tolerate this.

Proverbs 22:22-23 Expanded Bible (EXB)
Do not ·abuse [steal from] poor people because they are poor, and do not ·take away the rights of [oppress] the needy in ·court [the gate]. The LORD will ·defend them in court [accuse their accusers] and will ·take the life of those who take away their rights[press/squeeze the life out of those who press/squeeze them].

Strong's Concordance defines afflicted as:
depressed, in mind or circumstances: —afflicted, humble, lowly, needy, poor

Poor and afflicted is not just sick or homeless people although they are included, but they are people who are in need and going through challenges of life as well. They are people who are crying out to God just like you to shift situations and circumstances in their lives around. They are tired but giving all they have.

This scripture says do not abuse and take from them for your own gain. If you do God will take the life (soul, self, life, creature, person, appetite, mind, living being, desire, emotion, passion) away from the person who decided to abuse the poor. Whewww personally, I do not want to be on the end of that.

There are plenty of moguls that we could list that this mentality has seemingly worked for, but prosperity is much more than money. Money is only one aspect of true prosperity so although money for them is flourishing they may lack fulfillment, contentment, joy, peace, and protection from the ever-changing economy. It also important to know that prosperity is a generational blessing as well. True prosperity cannot come with blood on your hands. Our top priority as kingdom heirs is to be mindful of the hearts and souls of God's people. If you are stepping on the backs of others the blood is on your hands and there is no way for full prosperity to operate in your lives.

When you are fearful of what is next or how to make ends meet it can open up all of these doors. Here are some areas to cleanse and repent of during your prayer time:

- Take time to cleanse from fear and repent for any way you have abused the poor and afflicted and any hardship that was caused.
- Cleanse from any way you personally have been poor, afflicted, and abused. Break powers of the victim that would try to operate in your life.
- Cleanse and gut out all fear of lack and command the fullness of prosperity to enmesh with the truth of who God says you are. Break any restrictions/constrictions that you have placed on your finances because fear.
- Repent for any way you have mispositioned money in your life and exalted it above the provision of God.
- Cleanse your identity and personality from any place that has been enmeshed in fear of lack and fill each space with the blood and fire of Jesus.

WHO I AM IN CHRIST JESUS
(Author: Unknown)

1. I am God's child for I am born of the incorruptible seed of the Word of God which lives and abides forever (1Peter 1:23)

2. I am forgiven of all my sins and washed in the blood of Jesus (Ephesians 1:7; Hebrews 9:14; Colossians 1:14; 1 John 1:9; 1 John 2:12)

3. I am a new creature (2 Corinthians 5:17)

4. I am the temple of the Holy Spirit (1 Corinthians 6:19)

5. I am delivered from the power of darkness and translated into the Kingdom of God (Colossians 1:13)

6. I am redeemed from the curse of the Law (1Peter 1:18-19, Galatians 3:13)

7. I am blessed (Deuteronomy 28:1-4; Galatians 3:9)

8. I am a saint (Romans 1:7; 1 Corinthians 1:2; Philippians 1:1)

9. I am the head and not the tail (Deuteronomy 28:13)

10. I am holy and without blame before Him in love (1 Peter 1:16; Ephesians 1:4)

11. I am elect (Colossians 3:12; Romans 8:33)

12. I am established to the end (1 Corinthians 1:8)

13. I am made nigh by the blood of Christ (Ephesians 2:13)

14. I am victorious (Revelations 21:7)

15. I am made free (John 8:31-33)

16. I am strong in the Lord (Ephesians 6:10)

17. I am dead to sin (Romans 6:2, Romans 6:11; 1 Peter 2:24)

18. I am more than a conqueror (Romans 8:37)

19. I am joint heir with Christ (Romans 8:17)

20. I am sealed with the Holy Spirit of promise (Ephesians 1:13)

21. I am in Christ Jesus by His doing (1 Corinthians 1:30)

22. I am accepted in the Beloved (Ephesians 1:6)

23. I am complete in Him (Colossians 2:10)

24. I am crucified with Christ (Galatians 2:20)

25. I am alive with Christ (Ephesians 2:5)

26. I am free from condemnation (Romans 8:1)

27. I am reconciled to God (2 Corinthians 5:18)

28. I am qualified to share in His inheritance (Colossians 1:12)

29. I am firmly rooted, built up, established in my faith and overflowing with gratitude (Colossians 2:7)

30. I am circumcised with a circumcision made without hands (Colossians 2:11)

31. I am a fellow citizen of the saints and of the household of God (Ephesians 2:19)

32. I am built upon the foundation of the apostles and prophets, Jesus Christ Himself being the chief Cornerstone (Ephesians 2:20)

33. I am in the world as He is in Heaven (1John 4:17)

34. I am born of God and the evil one does not touch me (1 John 5:18)

35. I am His faithful follower (Revelation 17:14b; Ephesians 5:11)

36. I am overtaken with blessings (Deuteronomy 28:2; Ephesians 1:3)

37. I am His disciple because I have love for others (John 13:34-35)

38. I am the light of the world (Matthew 5:14)

39. I am the salt of the earth (Matthew 5:13)

40. I am the righteousness of God (2 Corinthians 5:21; 1 Peter 2:24)
    I am partaker of His divine nature (2 Peter 1:4)

42. I am called of God (2 Timothy 1:9)

43. I am the first fruit among His creation (James 1:18)

44. I am chosen (1 Thessalonians 1:4; Ephesians 1:4; 1 Peter 2:9)

45. I am an ambassador for Christ (2 Corinthians 5:20)

46. I am God's workmanship created in Christ for good works (Ephesians 2:10)

47. I am the apple of my Father's eye (Deuteronomy 32:10; Psalms 17:8)

48. I am healed by the stripes of Jesus (1 Peter 2:24; Isaiah 53:4)

49. I am being changed unto His image (2 Corinthians 3:18; Philippians 1:16)

50. I am raised up with Christ and seated in heavenly places (Ephesians 2:6)

51. I have obtained an inheritance (Ephesians 1:11)

52. I have access by one Spirit unto the Father (Hebrews 4:16; Ephesians 2:18)

53. I have overcome the world (1 John 5:4)

54. I have everlasting life and will not be condemned (John 5:24; John 5:47)

55. I have the peace of God which passes all understanding (Philippians 4:7)

56. I have received a down payment (earnest) of the Spirit of God (2 Corinthians 1:22; 2 Corinthians 5:5; Ephesians 1:13-14)

57. I have received power; power to lay hands on the sick and see them recover; power to cast out demons, power and authority to trample upon serpents and scorpions and over all the power of the enemy and nothing shall by any means hurt me (Mark 16:17-18b; Luke 10:17,19)

58. I live by and in the law of the Spirit of life in Christ Jesus which made me free from the law of sin and death (Romans 8:2 — also, read all of Romans chapter 8)

59. I live by faith in Christ (Galatians 2:20; 2 Corinthians 5:7)

60. I walk in the Spirit (Galatians 5:16)

61. I can do all things through Christ Jesus (Philippians 4:13)

62. My life is hid with Christ in God (Colossians 3:3)

63. I shall do even greater works than Christ Jesus (John 14:12)

64. I press toward the mark for the prize of the High calling of God (Philippians 3:14)

65. I possess the Greater One in me because greater is He who is in me than he who is in the world (1 John 4:4)

66. I am God's anointed one in Christ Jesus (2 Corinthians 1:21; 1 John 2:20, 27)

67. I always triumph in Christ (2 Corinthians 2:14)

68. I show forth His praises (1 Peter 2:9)

I PRACTICE ALL OF THE ABOVE SCRIPTURES WITHOUT FAIL, AND I WILL NEVER FAIL OR FAINT.

Strategic Sowing

The purpose for sowing in the natural is for growth. When we sow seed into the land our expectation is that the plant or crop will grow, and we will be able to utilize it. When it comes to financial sowing, the same principal can be utilized. We cannot give or sow into everything because our expectation should be that whatever we sow into should grow and produce lasting fruit.

> *Luke 8:5-8 English Standard Version (ESV)*
> *"A sower went out to sow his seed. And as he sowed, some fell along the path and was trampled underfoot, and the birds of the air devoured it. And some fell on the rock, and as it grew up, it withered away, because it had no moisture. And some fell among thorns, and the thorns grew up with it and choked it. And some fell into good soil and grew and yielded a hundredfold." As he said these things, he called out, "He who has ears to hear, let him hear."*

This scripture shows us that sowing in the right place and environment will produce the harvest a hundredfold. We also notice in this scripture that there were seeds that fell and were devoured so they never produced what was in them. Every seed we have carries a purpose and reason and if it falls on the wrong ground it may never produce or spring forth what is inside of it. This scripture also shows us that some seed fell among the thorns and was choked out. Sowing into the wrong environment can cause the very thing in us to be aborted. Sowing into "good ground" allows what is in us to flourish. When we sow we have to ask ourselves is this good ground and will it produce a hundredfold of what was sown? We may also want to ask God what is the purpose of this seed so that we can declare that the seed not only flourishes but brings forth in fullness all that God intended.

Often when I ask people why they decided to sow into an organization, foundation, or a ministry their response is that the spill that was given to them wooed them or they just thought it was a good cause. When we are a strategic sower these explanations cannot be the intentions for why we sow. Although these may be great causes and great ideas being intentional means there is a greater purpose for which we sow. We recognize that the seed we sow is intended to produce fruit. We do not want our seeds to fall on ground where it cannot be watered or grow. We recognize that our seed carries purpose and we are willing to make sure that our seed is not wasted.

There are various reasons why we may sow, and it is important to be clear on what we are sowing into, why we are sowing into it, and where our heart is when we sow so that you can recognize the fruit.

> *Galatians 6:7-10 The Message (MSG)*
> *Don't be misled: No one makes a fool of God. What a person plants, he will harvest. The person who plants selfishness, ignoring the needs of others – ignoring God! – harvests a crop of weeds. All he'll have to show for his life is weeds! But the one who plants in response to God, letting God's Spirit do the growth work in him, harvests a crop of real life, eternal life.*

So let's not allow ourselves to get fatigued doing good. At the right time we will harvest a good crop if we don't give up, or quit. Right now, therefore, every time we get the chance, let us work for the benefit of all, starting with the people closest to us in the community of faith.

This scripture lets us know that our heart's posture to God and adhering to his guidance and instruction is key to producing harvest that is lasting. Part of the growth process in finances and in our household is allowing God to do a work in us that will change our mindset and perceptions of things. Truly allowing God to lead our sowing yields our control to him and positions him above our finances thus allowing the blessings of God to flow in our lives.

Financially we all expect a return on our investment weather we are operating from the secular marketplace or within a ministry. If we sow into organizations, ministries, churches, or even certain items without knowing the foundation, we are sowing in the dark and hoping for a return instead of expecting it, thus opening the door to false expectations. If you have no idea of the ground that we have sown or invested into we will reap but will it be what we thought? The truth of what you have sown into will produce but not knowing what that is could mean that you have come into agreement with something you never would have intended to grow. It is important that we become cognizant of these things so that we truly create the standard we desire in our families, foundations, organizations, ministries, regions, and business systems.

The Beauty of Consistency

Consistency is an attribute of God and is something should reflect in our charter.

Dictionary.com defines consistency as:
1. *a degree of density, firmness, viscosity, etc*
2. **steadfast adherence to the same principles, course, form, etc**
3. *agreement, harmony, or compatibility, especially correspondence or uniformity among the parts of a complex thing*

Consistency leaves no room for indecisiveness but a steadfastness and a definite yes or no. It also allows us to be firmly rooted and unifies us with the father. Uniting with the father allows us to tap into the fullness of his resources. Colossians 1:17 tells us that all things are before him and all things are held together by him. In order to have sustainability we must be consistent in him so that he can be consistent in us and through us.

Corinthians 15:58 English Standard Version (ESV)
Therefore, my beloved brothers, be steadfast, immovable, always abounding in the work of the Lord, knowing that in the Lord your labor is not in vain.

Matthew 5:37 English Standard Version (ESV)
Let what you say be simply 'Yes' or 'No'; anything more than this comes from evil.

Colossians 1:17 Good News Translation (GNT)
Christ existed before all things, and in union with him all things have their proper place.

As we begin to lay out the kingdom plan for our households and finances consistency is a tool that we can utilize. We become accountable for the plan and perfected in the processing of the plan for our household and finances and we unify, submit, and align with it. It is only through him that we can truly stay consistent and not sway or shift from the plan he placed in us.

1 John 2:3-7 English Standard Version (ESV)

And by this we know that we have come to know him, if we keep his commandments. Whoever says "I know him" but does not keep his commandments is a liar, and the truth is not in him, but whoever keeps his word, in him truly the love of God is perfected. By this we may know that we are in him: whoever says he abides in him ought to walk in the same way in which he walked. Beloved, I am writing you no new commandment, but an old commandment that you had from the beginning. The old commandment is the word that you have heard.

If we find that we are not sticking with the plans and the changes made were not by God's instruction, we want to get deliverance in any areas that would rebel against the instruction and word of God. Command the fire of God to burn up everything that is not like God and attempting to exalt itself against the instructions of God.

Benefits of Consistency

Consistency allows for measurement.
Being consistent will allow you to be able to analyze your finances and be more strategic and effective in the plans that are put together for your household and finances month to month and even annually.

Consistency creates accountability.
Being accountable helps track progress but also allows is a place of resource and truth so that you stay on the right track in spite of challenges that may arise

Consistency makes you creditable.
Consistency allows you to build that predictable flow that people can see and thus making what you say carry weight and creating a reputation of relevancy. Having creditability and relevancy can open up different streams of income and investments for you and your household thus helping to further secure your financial freedom.

Consistency makes you committed.
Being committed to God relinquishes personal control and puts your trust in him as a father to provide, cover and protect you. Being committed also allows inheritance and blessings flow on your behalf.

Committing to the process allows the changes that need to be made in old mindsets and behaviors to take place, while perfecting in you what he desires from you in the area of finances. These changes help solidify who God is in you, while showing you how to remain realistic in your budgeting for your household and evaluating it through the proper wells so that as changes in the economy occur the basic foundations have been rooted in you and assist in shielding against negative or adverse changes.

The Beauty of Consistency Prayer

(By Amanda Latrice)

Lord we open ourselves up in the deep places of our hearts today. We repent for not reflecting your character by being inconsistent. We repent for not letting our yes be yes and no be no. We repent for anyway we have swayed from the plan and vision you have given us for our household and finances. Fire of God, we give you full access to set ablaze every place attached to inconsistency, instability, lukewarmness, and discord right now in the name of Jesus. We declare that the word, plan, and execution of what you have said father will go forth. We repent for any way inconsistency has closed up the fruit of prosperity from operating in our lives. Lord God cleanse every place by fire and purge it with your blood that we would bare your fruit. We break every tie we have with inconsistency and renounce any rights and access that we have given. We shut down its operations in our lives, our household, and our generations right now in the name of Jesus. We speak healing to the places in us that cause us to be fearful of operating in consistency father. We cleanse out all discouragement, pain of the past, and fear right now in the name of Jesus. We declare the healing and cleansing power of God is overtaking us right now in the name of Jesus.

We love your consistency father and we desire to give you full commitment in the things that you have required for our finances and household. We open ourselves up all the more and say come and infuse our character, personality, identity, and habits in your constituency. We shift into abiding consistently in you and being filled by you in this season. As we commit to you father we declare that:

- We will have consistency in all that we will put our hands to and will finish what we start.
- We will continuously produce measurable fruit in our finances and household
- We will be firmly rooted in your plans and not be swayed.
- We will be accountable to those assigned in our lives to help us stay consistent

We want our consistency to be a reflection of you father. We declare we want the fullness of your prosperity in this season and we yield ourselves to the instructions, guidance, plans, and accountability that you have released in this season.

We declare are firmly rooted in you father and consistent in the things of you. You can trust us with your plans that you desire for your family and sphere of influence. We command consistency to rise up in us this hour and anytime inconsistency would try to manifest a holy conviction would come upon us to shift us back into focus.
We shift to fully operating in your consistency father....this we commit to you. In Jesus Name, Amen.

Sowing and Reaping

Operating from a Kingdom Perspective

The kingdom of God is a system of operation that is governed by specific spiritual laws. For us to reap from the kingdom, we must be proficient in knowing how it operates. The Kingdom of God is under the rule and dominion of the Lord, and because we are kingdom heirs and we birth forth from this kingdom all rights and privileges of the kingdom of God have been conferred upon us…. but what are those rights and privileges? What are his laws?

Righteousness
Matt 6:33 says, *But seek first the kingdom of God and his righteousness, and all these things will be added to you.*

Seek in this scripture means:
1. To crave, put a demand on, require, aim at or strive.

Righteousness means:
2. Integrity, virtue, purity of life, rightness, correctness of thinking feeling, and acting
3. in a narrower sense, justice or the virtue which gives each his due

Virtue:
Is comparable to a great army, to power, strength, and fortitude of army soldiers, and it has all the riches and the resources we need to maintain the standard of God (Apostle Taquetta Baker).

Righteousness is a key component to the laws and regulations of the kingdom. Correct set up and order allows a structure to be developed where we can build an expectation of cause and effect or sowing and reaping. When we crave and put a demand on the purity, integrity, virtue, and correctness of our finances, then our heart becomes postured in a place where our intentions are aligned with God, and when we sow it is strategic and intentional thus activating the scriptures that all these things well be added unto you.

Questions to search out:
1. What are you seeking after concerning your finances (craving, putting a demand, require, aim or strive)?
2. Is what you seek what after in line with the righteousness of God? If not what areas of your finances lack the righteousness of God?
3. Is your heart postured in a way that it can receive the righteousness God so that you can carry the mandate and vision for your household or business? If not, ask God to begin to deal with the posture of your heart concerning finances.
4. Pray and ask God to begin to cultivate those areas and produce a deep craving where your heart for your finances align with his heart for your finances.

Dominion

Genesis 1:26&28
And God said, Let us make man in our image, after our likeness: and let them have dominion over the fish of the sea, and over the fowl of the air, and over the cattle, and over all the earth, and over every creeping thing that creepeth upon the earth. And God blessed them, and God said unto them, Be fruitful, and multiply, and replenish the earth, and subdue it: and have dominion over the fish of the sea, and over the fowl of the air, and over every living thing that moveth upon the earth.

Subdue in that scripture means:
To bring under cultivation.

Because we are made in the image of God dominion is not just about commanding but it's an actual characteristic that allow us to scrape out, govern, and cultivate, thus bringing about God's sovereign authority in our sphere of influence. To have dominion over the finances we must embrace the truth of who we are as a child and heir of the king.

Let us make in this scripture means:
1. to do, fashion, accomplish, make
    1. (Qal)
        1. to do, work, make, produce
            1. to do
            2. to work
            3. to deal (with)
            4. to act, act with effect, effect
        2. to make
            1. to make
            2. to produce
            3. to prepare
            4. to make (an offering)
            5. to attend to, put in order
            6. to observe, celebrate
            7. to acquire (property)
            8. to appoint, ordain, institute
            9. to bring about
            10. to use
            11. to spend, pass
            12. to put in the proper state

When God decided to make us in his image he literally put on the inside of us the ability and characteristics of himself. He appointed and ordained us to operate from a pure state that reflects his heart and desire for us, our family, our business, our organization, our ministry and all that concerns us. He fashioned it in our very DNA. His very standard is what he spoke over us from the very beginning. To operate from the place of dominion we must fully embrace that we were formed, fashioned, and appointed to govern and make sure that the standard of God is the only thing reigning in our sphere of influence. When we recognize this, we become more intentional about where we sow, what we sow, and how we sow as it determines what is allowed with in our regions and sphere of influence. I am sure most think this is only for businesses, but the reality is families and households hold the key to what is operable in our regions. What our households in our regions sow into shows what we will and will not allow in our regions. Shifting into true dominion will allow us to create the standard of God for households thus effecting our regions and all that concern us. Embracing dominion as part of who we are all will allow the truth of who God fashioned and formed to come forth in our households and put a demand on the fullness of God for our families financially and in general.

Law of Reciprocity

The Law of Reciprocity is cause and effect (i.e., if you sow you will reap). Let's look at the law of reciprocity as it relates to sowing and what keys components are in the scriptures that help us determine when we are sowing in alignment with what God requires for our lives.

Malachi 3:10 King James Version (KJV)
¹⁰ Bring ye all the tithes into the storehouse, that there may be meat in mine house, and prove me now herewith, saith the LORD of hosts, if I will not open you the windows of heaven, and pour you out a blessing, that there shall not be room enough to receive it.

Malachi 3:10 English Standard Version (ESV)

¹⁰ Bring the full tithe into the storehouse, that there may be food in my house. And thereby put me to the test, says the LORD of hosts, if I will not open the windows of heaven for you and pour down for you a blessing until there is no more need.

We often hear this scripture in reference to the reason why we should tithe to our church but there are keys that lets us know what we should actually be sowing into.

Storehouse in this scripture means:
Treasure house and God's armory (a building in which training in the use of arms and drill takes place; drill hall) - a secure place for the storage of weapons.

When we sow one of the questions we must ask is am I sowing into my training ground? Am I sowing into the place that God has chosen to create a secure environment for me to learn who I am, learn my weapons, and train? Often time we assume this means our church, but it is actually the place and even person used to train and cultivate us, so that food is available, or weaponry is available for training us as well as others. This is not to say your church is not feeding you, but we must expand our mind past just sowing into a church to receive a blessing and truly being intentional in sowing into the very places, people, and ministries that help train and cultivate our very identity and destiny.

Proverbs 3:9-10 King James Version (KJV)
Honour the LORD with thy substance, and with the first fruits of all thine increase:
So shall thy barns be filled with plenty, and thy presses shall burst out with new wine.

Proverbs 3: 9-10 (Message Version)
Honor GOD with everything you own; give him the first and the best.
Your barns will burst, your wine vats will brim over.

Substance in this scripture is not only money or produce, but it's anything with high value. If we consider it an increase or a blessing added to our lives it needs to remain yielded to Him.

In this scripture first fruits means the best part. This is another scripture that we hear in reference to tithing but truly this scripture tells us that anything that has added value or increase in our lives we are being asked to honor God with. This requires a lifestyle not just funds but a complete yielding of who we are and all that is added to us. This scripture lets us know that as we honor God with the first fruits and sow strategically and intentionally the effect is that we will be filled to full and overflow. Just as he is requiring a lifestyle yielded his effect is to fill every place including your finances, but not limited to your finances. When we create the lifestyle of life poured out to him he becomes limitless in what he can do for us and through us.

Points to remember:
1. Sowing and reaping is a spiritual process in which spiritual guidelines must be followed.
2. The law of sowing and reaping must be a lifestyle that is yielded to the purpose and plan of God.
3. We must be willing to sow in all seasons and with strategy and trust the truth of what the Lord says would happen if we follow his laws and abide in his government.

Monthly Bill Tracker

List your bills, the due date, and amount. Once you have paid the bill for the month check it off.

Bill Description	Due Date	Amount	Jan	Feb	Mar	Apr	May	Jun	Jul	Aug	Sep	Oct	Nov	Dec
			☐	☐	☐	☐	☐	☐	☐	☐	☐	☐	☐	☐
			☐	☐	☐	☐	☐	☐	☐	☐	☐	☐	☐	☐
			☐	☐	☐	☐	☐	☐	☐	☐	☐	☐	☐	☐
			☐	☐	☐	☐	☐	☐	☐	☐	☐	☐	☐	☐
			☐	☐	☐	☐	☐	☐	☐	☐	☐	☐	☐	☐
			☐	☐	☐	☐	☐	☐	☐	☐	☐	☐	☐	☐
			☐	☐	☐	☐	☐	☐	☐	☐	☐	☐	☐	☐
			☐	☐	☐	☐	☐	☐	☐	☐	☐	☐	☐	☐
			☐	☐	☐	☐	☐	☐	☐	☐	☐	☐	☐	☐
			☐	☐	☐	☐	☐	☐	☐	☐	☐	☐	☐	☐
			☐	☐	☐	☐	☐	☐	☐	☐	☐	☐	☐	☐
			☐	☐	☐	☐	☐	☐	☐	☐	☐	☐	☐	☐
			☐	☐	☐	☐	☐	☐	☐	☐	☐	☐	☐	☐
			☐	☐	☐	☐	☐	☐	☐	☐	☐	☐	☐	☐
			☐	☐	☐	☐	☐	☐	☐	☐	☐	☐	☐	☐
			☐	☐	☐	☐	☐	☐	☐	☐	☐	☐	☐	☐
			☐	☐	☐	☐	☐	☐	☐	☐	☐	☐	☐	☐
			☐	☐	☐	☐	☐	☐	☐	☐	☐	☐	☐	☐
			☐	☐	☐	☐	☐	☐	☐	☐	☐	☐	☐	☐
			☐	☐	☐	☐	☐	☐	☐	☐	☐	☐	☐	☐
			☐	☐	☐	☐	☐	☐	☐	☐	☐	☐	☐	☐
			☐	☐	☐	☐	☐	☐	☐	☐	☐	☐	☐	☐
			☐	☐	☐	☐	☐	☐	☐	☐	☐	☐	☐	☐
			☐	☐	☐	☐	☐	☐	☐	☐	☐	☐	☐	☐
			☐	☐	☐	☐	☐	☐	☐	☐	☐	☐	☐	☐

MONTH 1

Monthly *Income*

Date Received	Income Amount
Monthly Total:	

Monthly Utilities *Expense*

Date	Description	Amount	Balance

Monthly Transportation *Expense*

Date	Description	Amount	Balance

Monthly Household *Expense*

Date	Description	Amount	Balance

Monthly Giving

Date	Description	Amount	Balance

Monthly Dinning *Expense*

Date	Description	Amount	Balance

Monthly Entertainment *Expense*

Date	Description	Amount	Balance

Monthly Kids *Expense*

Date	Description	Amount	Balance

Monthly Miscellaneous *Expense*

Date	Description	Amount	Balance

Monthly SAVINGS

Date	Amount Saved	Balance

Debt Plan

Date	Description	Amount	Balance

MONTH AT A GLANCE

The Month Of : _____

Starting Bal: _____

Expenses/Bills | Income/Extras

Mortgage _____

Utilities _____

Transportation _____

Household Expenses _____

Dinning _____

Entertainment _____

Health Insurance _____

Kids _____

Giving _____
Miscellaneous _____

Total Expenses:

Income from Work : _____

Other Income (List):

_____   _____

_____   _____

_____   _____

_____   _____

Savings:

_____   _____

Total Income:

Ending Balance:

Month End Reflection:

1. Take a look at your Monthly expenses detail sheets. List in order (from most expensive to least expensive) your expenses.

_____
_____
_____
_____
_____
_____
_____
_____
_____
_____

2. Take a look at your Monthly expenses detail Sheets. In what areas can you reduce your spending?

_____
_____
_____
_____
_____
_____
_____
_____
_____

3. Is there additional funds that you can put in your savings account? If so how much? How much are you willing to put in your savings Next Month?

_____
_____
_____
_____
_____

4. Are there any funds that can be directed towards your debt? If so how much can you add to a monthly bill next month?

_____
_____
_____
_____

5. **Monthly Goals:** Using the information from your reflection along with your Month at a glance sheet fill in your goals/estimated budget amounts for next month.

Expenses/Bills	Income/Extras
Mortgage _____	Income from Work: _____
Utilities _____	
Transportation _____	Other Income (List):
Household Expenses _____	_____ _____
Dinning _____	_____ _____
Entertainment _____	_____ _____
Health Insurance _____	_____ _____
Kids _____	Savings: _____ _____
Giving _____	
Miscellaneous _____	**Total Income:**
Total Expenses:	

36 | Page

MONTH 2

Prosperity Focus

Honour
The Lord
With YOur

Substance!

I choose to honour God in every area of my life including my finances. I choose to make sure that he is pleased with how I spend my finances. It is important that I please God with everything he has granted to my hands. My heart father is that you be Honoured

Proverbs 3:9

Monthly *Income*

Date Received	Income Amount
Monthly Total:	

Monthly Utilities *Expense*

Date	Description	Amount	Balance

Monthly Transportation *Expense*

Date	Description	Amount	Balance

Monthly Household *Expense*

Date	Description	Amount	Balance

Monthly Dinning *Expense*

Date	Description	Amount	Balance

Monthly Entertainment *Expense*

Date	Description	Amount	Balance

Monthly Kids *Expense*

Date	Description	Amount	Balance

Monthly Miscellaneous *Expense*

Date	Description	Amount	Balance

Monthly *SAVINGS*

Date	Amount Saved	Balance

Debt Plan

Date	Description	Amount	Balance

MONTH AT A GLANCE

The Month Of: _____

Starting Bal: [_____]

Expenses/Bills	Income/Extras
Mortgage _____	Income from Work: _____
Utilities _____	
Transportation _____	Other Income (List):
Household Expenses _____	_____ _____
Dinning _____	_____ _____
Entertainment _____	_____ _____
Health Insurance _____	_____ _____
Kids _____	Savings: _____ _____
Giving _____	
Miscellaneous _____	Total Income:
Total Expenses:	[_____]

Ending Balance:

[_____]

Month End Reflection:

1. Take a look at your Monthly expenses detail sheets. List in order (from most expensive to least expensive) your expenses.

___

2. Take a look at your Monthly expenses detail Sheets. In what areas can you reduce your spending?

___

3. Is there additional funds that you can put in your savings account? If so how much? How much are you willing to put in your savings Next Month?

_____
_____
_____
_____
_____

4. Are there any funds that can be directed towards your debt? If so how much can you add to a monthly bill next month?

_____
_____
_____
_____
_____

5. **Monthly Goals:** Using the information from your reflection along with your Month at a glance sheet fill in your goals/estimated budget amounts for next month.

Expenses/Bills	Income/Extras
Mortgage _____	Income from Work: _____
Utilities _____	
Transportation _____	Other Income (List):
Household Expenses _____	_____ _____
Dinning _____	_____ _____
Entertainment _____	_____ _____
Health Insurance _____	
Kids _____	Savings:
Giving _____	_____ _____
Miscellaneous _____	**Total Income:**
Total Expenses:	

MONTH 3

AND MY GOD
WILL MEET ALL MY NEEDS
ACCORDING TO HIS

GLORIOUS

RICHES

IN CHRIST JESUS

PHILLIPPIANS 4:9

Monthly *Income*

Date Received	Income Amount
Monthly Total:	

Monthly Utilities *Expense*

Date	Description	Amount	Balance

Monthly Transportation *Expense*

Date	Description	Amount	Balance

Monthly Household *Expense*

Date	Description	Amount	Balance

Monthly Giving

Date	Description	Amount	Balance

Monthly Dinning *Expense*

Date	Description	Amount	Balance

Monthly Entertainment *Expense*

Date	Description	Amount	Balance

Monthly Kids *Expense*

Date	Description	Amount	Balance

Monthly Miscellaneous *Expense*

Date	Description	Amount	Balance

Monthly SAVINGS

Date	Amount Saved	Balance

Debt Plan

Date	Description	Amount	Balance

MONTH AT A GLANCE

The Month Of : _____

Starting Bal: _____

Expenses/Bills | Income/Extras

Mortgage _____

Utilities _____

Transportation _____

Household Expenses _____

Dinning _____

Entertainment _____

Health Insurance _____

Kids _____

Giving _____

Miscellaneous _____

Total Expenses:

Income from Work: _____

Other Income (List):

_____   _____

_____   _____

_____   _____

_____   _____

Savings:

_____   _____

Total Income:

Ending Balance:

End Reflection:

1. Take a look at your Monthly expenses detail sheets. List in order (from most expensive to least expensive) your expenses.

___

2. Take a look at your Monthly expenses detail Sheets. In what areas can you reduce your spending?

___

3. Is there additional funds that you can put in your savings account? If so how much? How much are you willing to put in your savings Next Month?

_____
_____
_____
_____
_____

4. Are there any funds that can be directed towards your debt? If so how much can you add to a monthly bill next month?

_____
_____
_____
_____
_____

5. **Monthly Goals:** Using the information from your reflection along with your Month at a glance sheet fill in your goals/estimated budget amounts for next month.

Expenses/Bills	Income/Extras
Mortgage _____	Income from Work: _____
Utilities _____	
Transportation _____	Other Income (List):
Household Expenses _____	_____ _____
Dinning _____	_____ _____
Entertainment _____	_____ _____
Health Insurance _____	_____ _____
Kids _____	Savings: _____ _____
Giving _____	
Miscellaneous _____	**Total Income:**
Total Expenses:	

MONTH 4

Household Budgeting Declaration

(By Amanda Latrice)

We declare that our households, business, and families belong to GOD. We declare that we are administrators and stewards of your kingdom prosperity. As we budget we do it with a clear focus of what you are speaking for our households and generations.

We declare that our households are producing resources and blessings to help finance and sustain the visions that God has given us.

We declare that the spirts of poverty, lack, fear, and intimidation that would try to attack our household is bound and cast out of our generational line.

We declare that the spirit of compromise has no right in our household, on our land, or in us…..It is being cleansed out right now in the name of Jesus.

We declare that we are fortified in God's truth and we will not allow the lies of enemy from the past or the present to go any further in us or our generations.

We declare that all sabotaging spirits that would try to operate in the finances of our household are broken in the name of Jesus.

We declare that our generations are being cleansed of all impure motives, competition, pride, deceitfulness, manipulation, covetousness, and they are being fortified in life, purity, love, fruitfulness, success, and abundance right now in the name of Jesus.

We declare that our household will only sow seeds and cultivate in the areas that God tells us to sow into.

We declare that we are strategic stewards of our finances and we operate from a kingdom perspective only.

We declare our household is fruitful.

We declare our household is successful.

We declare our household is prosperous.

We declare our household is receiving heavenly wisdom that will cause alignment to our finances and all that concerns us.

We declare healing to every wound that has been caused by financial hardship and we call forth a cleansing of those areas now in the name of Jesus.

We declare we will not operate from an old or wounded well but we will operate with a kingdom perspective.

We declare our household and generations are shifting back to the ruler ship and direction of the almighty God.

We declare our family is producing and reproducing as we align with the word, truth, and strategy of God for our finances and households.

We declare it and establish it in us and our generations and it is a continuous work.
In Jesus name, Amen

Monthly *Income*

Date Received	Income Amount
Monthly Total:	

Monthly Utilities *Expense*

Date	Description	Amount	Balance

Monthly Transportation *Expense*

Date	Description	Amount	Balance

Monthly Household *Expense*

Date	Description	Amount	Balance

Monthly Giving

Date	Description	Amount	Balance

Monthly Dinning *Expense*

Date	Description	Amount	Balance

Monthly Entertainment *Expense*

Date	Description	Amount	Balance

Monthly Kids *Expense*

Date	Description	Amount	Balance

Monthly Miscellaneous *Expense*

Date	Description	Amount	Balance

Monthly *SAVINGS*

Date	Amount Saved	Balance

Debt Plan

Date	Description	Amount	Balance

MONTH AT A GLANCE

The Month Of: _____

Starting Bal: [_____]

Expenses/Bills	Income/Extras
Mortgage _____	Income from Work: _____
Utilities _____	
Transportation _____	Other Income (List):
Household Expenses _____	_____ _____
Dinning _____	_____ _____
Entertainment _____	_____ _____
Health Insurance _____	_____ _____
Kids _____	Savings:
Giving _____	_____ _____
Miscellaneous _____	**Total Income:**
Total Expenses:	

Ending Balance:

Month End Reflection:

1. Take a look at your Monthly expenses detail sheets. List in order (from most expensive to least expensive) your expenses.

_____
_____
_____
_____
_____
_____
_____
_____

2. Take a look at your Monthly expenses detail Sheets. In what areas can you reduce your spending?

_____
_____
_____
_____
_____
_____
_____
_____

3. Is there additional funds that you can put in your savings account? If so how much? How much are you willing to put in your savings Next Month?

_____

_____

_____

_____

_____

4. Are there any funds that can be directed towards your debt? If so how much can you add to a monthly bill next month?

_____

_____

_____

_____

_____

5. **Monthly Goals:** Using the information from your reflection along with your Month at a glance sheet fill in your goals/estimated budget amounts for next month.

Expenses/Bills	Income/Extras
Mortgage _____	Income from Work: _____
Utilities _____	
Transportation _____	Other Income (List):
Household Expenses _____	_____ _____
Dinning _____	_____ _____
Entertainment _____	_____ _____
Health Insurance _____	_____ _____
Kids _____	Savings: _____ _____
Giving _____	
Miscellaneous _____	
Total Expenses:	**Total Income:**

MONTH 5

Monthly *Income*

Date Received	Income Amount
Monthly Total:	

Prosperity Focus

Proverbs 14:23

Hard Work pays off; mere talk puts no on bread on the table

I declare that I am not just talking but I am walking this thing out. My actions will and are aligning with what God has said for me and my household.

Monthly Utilities *Expense*

Date	Description	Amount	Balance

Monthly Transportation *Expense*

Date	Description	Amount	Balance

Monthly Household *Expense*

Date	Description	Amount	Balance

Monthly Giving

Date	Description	Amount	Balance

Monthly Dinning *Expense*

Date	Description	Amount	Balance

Monthly Entertainment *Expense*

Date	Description	Amount	Balance

Monthly Kids *Expense*

Date	Description	Amount	Balance

Monthly Miscellaneous *Expense*

Date	Description	Amount	Balance

Monthly SAVINGS

Date	Amount Saved	Balance

Debt Plan

Date	Description	Amount	Balance

MONTH AT A GLANCE

The Month Of: _____

Starting Bal: [   ]

Expenses/Bills

Mortgage _____

Utilities _____

Transportation _____

Household Expenses _____

Dinning _____

Entertainment _____

Health Insurance _____

Kids _____

Giving _____

Miscellaneous _____

Total Expenses:

Income/Extras

Income from Work: _____

Other Income (List):

_____   _____

_____   _____

_____   _____

_____   _____

Savings:

_____   _____

Total Income:

Ending Balance:

Month End Reflection:

1. Take a look at your Monthly expenses detail sheets. List in order (from most expensive to least expensive) your expenses.

___

2. Take a look at your Monthly expenses detail Sheets. In what areas can you reduce your spending?

___

3. Is there additional funds that you can put in your savings account? If so how much? How much are you willing to put in your savings Next Month?

_____
_____
_____
_____
_____

4. Are there any funds that can be directed towards your debt? If so how much can you add to a monthly bill next month?

_____
_____
_____
_____
_____

5. **Monthly Goals:** Using the information from your reflection along with your Month at a glance sheet fill in your goals/estimated budget amounts for next month.

Expenses/Bills	Income/Extras
Mortgage _____	Income from Work: _____
Utilities _____	
Transportation _____	Other Income (List):
Household Expenses _____	_____ _____
Dinning _____	_____ _____
Entertainment _____	_____ _____
Health Insurance _____	_____ _____
Kids _____	Savings: _____ _____
Giving _____	
Miscellaneous _____	
Total Expenses:	**Total Income:**

MONTH 6

Prosperity Focus

FINANCE IS ONLY AN

EXACT SCIENCE UNTIL A
HUMAN TOUCHES IT.

HOW YOU HANDLE

YOUR MONEY REFLECTS

WHO YOU ARE

DAVE RAMSEY

Monthly *Income*

Date Received	Income Amount
Monthly Total:	

Monthly Utilities *Expense*

Date	Description	Amount	Balance

Monthly Transportation *Expense*

Date	Description	Amount	Balance

Monthly Household *Expense*

Date	Description	Amount	Balance

Monthly Giving

Date	Description	Amount	Balance

Monthly Dinning *Expense*

Date	Description	Amount	Balance

Monthly Entertainment *Expense*

Date	Description	Amount	Balance

Monthly Kids *Expense*

Date	Description	Amount	Balance

Monthly Miscellaneous *Expense*

Date	Description	Amount	Balance

Monthly *SAVINGS*

Date	Amount Saved	Balance

Debt Plan

Date	Description	Amount	Balance

MONTH AT A GLANCE

The Month Of: _____

Starting Bal: [   ]

Expenses/Bills	Income/Extras
Mortgage _____	Income from Work: _____
Utilities _____	
Transportation _____	Other Income (List):
Household Expenses _____	_____ _____
Dinning _____	_____ _____
Entertainment _____	_____ _____
Health Insurance _____	_____ _____
Kids _____	Savings:
Giving _____	_____ _____
Miscellaneous _____	
Total Expenses:	**Total Income:**

Ending Balance:

[   ]

Month End Reflection:

1. Take a look at your Monthly expenses detail sheets. List in order (from most expensive to least expensive) your expenses.

_____
_____
_____
_____
_____
_____
_____
_____

2. Take a look at your Monthly expenses detail Sheets. In what areas can you reduce your spending?

_____
_____
_____
_____
_____
_____
_____
_____

3. Is there additional funds that you can put in your savings account? If so how much? How much are you willing to put in your savings Next Month?

_____
_____
_____
_____
_____

4. Are there any funds that can be directed towards your debt? If so how much can you add to a monthly bill next month?

_____
_____
_____
_____
_____

5. **Monthly Goals:** Using the information from your reflection along with your Month at a glance sheet fill in your goals/estimated budget amounts for next month.

Expenses/Bills	Income/Extras
Mortgage _____	Income from Work: _____
Utilities _____	
Transportation _____	Other Income (List):
Household Expenses _____	_____ _____
Dinning _____	_____ _____
Entertainment _____	_____ _____
Health Insurance _____	_____ _____
Kids _____	Savings: _____ _____
Giving _____	
Miscellaneous _____	**Total Income:**
Total Expenses:	

MONTH 7

Prosperity Focus

Dishonest Money Dwindles Away

But Whoever Gathers Money Little By Little

Make It Grow

Proverbs 13:11

Monthly *Income*

Date Received	Income Amount
Monthly Total:	

Monthly Utilities *Expense*

Date	Description	Amount	Balance

Monthly Transportation *Expense*

Date	Description	Amount	Balance

Monthly Household *Expense*

Date	Description	Amount	Balance

Monthly Giving

Date	Description	Amount	Balance

Monthly Dinning *Expense*

Date	Description	Amount	Balance

Monthly Entertainment *Expense*

Date	Description	Amount	Balance

Monthly Kids *Expense*

Date	Description	Amount	Balance

Monthly Miscellaneous *Expense*

Date	Description	Amount	Balance

Monthly *SAVINGS*

Date	Amount Saved	Balance

Debt Plan

Date	Description	Amount	Balance

MONTH AT A GLANCE

The Month Of: _____

Starting Bal: [   ]

Expenses/Bills | Income/Extras

Expenses/Bills		Income/Extras
Mortgage	_____	Income from Work: _____
Utilities	_____	
Transportation	_____	Other Income (List):
Household Expenses	_____	_____ _____
Dinning	_____	_____ _____
Entertainment	_____	_____ _____
Health Insurance	_____	_____ _____
Kids	_____	Savings:
Giving	_____	_____ _____
Miscellaneous	_____	**Total Income:**
Total Expenses:		

Ending Balance:

[   ]

Month End Reflection:

1. Take a look at your Monthly expenses detail sheets. List in order (from most expensive to least expensive) your expenses.

_____
_____
_____
_____
_____
_____
_____
_____
_____
_____

2. Take a look at your Monthly expenses detail Sheets. In what areas can you reduce your spending?

_____
_____
_____
_____
_____
_____
_____
_____
_____
_____

3. Is there additional funds that you can put in your savings account? If so how much? How much are you willing to put in your savings Next Month?

_____
_____
_____
_____
_____

4. Are there any funds that can be directed towards your debt? If so how much can you add to a monthly bill next month?

_____
_____
_____
_____
_____

5. **Monthly Goals:** Using the information from your reflection along with your Month at a glance sheet fill in your goals/estimated budget amounts for next month.

Expenses/Bills	Income/Extras
Mortgage _____	Income from Work: _____
Utilities _____	
Transportation _____	Other Income (List):
Household Expenses _____	_____ _____
Dinning _____	_____ _____
Entertainment _____	_____ _____
Health Insurance _____	_____ _____
Kids _____	Savings: _____ _____
Giving _____	
Miscellaneous _____	**Total Income:**
Total Expenses:	

MONTH 8

Regional Authority Declaration

for Business Owners

(By Amanda Latrice)

We declare that our regions belong to GOD

We declare that our cities, states, and regions are receiving the businesses and ministries that God has given us.

We declare that our regions are producing resources and blessings to help finance and sustain the visions that God has given us.

We declare that the spirts of intimidation that would try to attack our kingdom businesses is bound and cast out of our region.

We declare that the spirit of compromise has no right in our region, on our land, or in us…..It is being cleansed out right now in the name of Jesus.

We declare that as kingdom entrepreneurs we are fortified in God's truth and we will not allow the lies of enemy from the past or the present to go any further in our regions or in us.

We declare that that the spirit of control that would try to dictate how our businesses should be developed is being judged now in the name of Jesus. Our business will be developed the way God says so!

We declare that our region is being cleansed of all impure motives, competition, pride, deceitfulness, manipulation, covetousness, and they are being fortified in life, purity, love, fruitfulness, success, and abundance right now in the name of Jesus.

We declare that our regions will only cultivate life to every God given vision in our sphere of influence.

We declare our region is fruitful

We declare our region is successful

We declare our region is shifting back to the ruler ship and direction of the almighty God.

We declare our regions know our name and our business' name and what we declare the region is producing and bring forth.

We declare it and establish it in our regions and it is a continuous work.
In Jesus name, Amen

Monthly *Income*

Date Received	Income Amount
Monthly Total:	

Monthly Utilities *Expense*

Date	Description	Amount	Balance

Monthly Transportation *Expense*

Date	Description	Amount	Balance

Monthly Household *Expense*

Date	Description	Amount	Balance

Monthly Giving

Date	Description	Amount	Balance

Monthly Dinning *Expense*

Date	Description	Amount	Balance

Monthly Entertainment *Expense*

Date	Description	Amount	Balance

Monthly Kids *Expense*

Date	Description	Amount	Balance

Monthly Miscellaneous *Expense*

Date	Description	Amount	Balance

Monthly *SAVINGS*

Date	Amount Saved	Balance

Debt Plan

Date	Description	Amount	Balance

MONTH AT A GLANCE

The Month Of: _____

Starting Bal: [_____]

Expenses/Bills	Income/Extras
Mortgage _____	Income from Work: _____
Utilities _____	
Transportation _____	Other Income (List):
Household Expenses _____	_____ _____
Dinning _____	_____ _____
Entertainment _____	_____ _____
Health Insurance _____	_____ _____
Kids _____	Savings: _____ _____
Giving _____	
Miscellaneous _____	**Total Income:**
Total Expenses:	

Ending Balance:

[_____]

Month End Reflection:

1. Take a look at your Monthly expenses detail sheets. List in order (from most expensive to least expensive) your expenses.

_____
_____
_____
_____
_____
_____
_____
_____

2. Take a look at your Monthly expenses detail Sheets. In what areas can you reduce your spending?

_____
_____
_____
_____
_____
_____
_____
_____

3. Is there additional funds that you can put in your savings account? If so how much? How much are you willing to put in your savings Next Month?

_____
_____
_____
_____
_____

4. Are there any funds that can be directed towards your debt? If so how much can you add to a monthly bill next month?

_____
_____
_____
_____
_____

5. **Monthly Goals:** Using the information from your reflection along with your Month at a glance sheet fill in your goals/estimated budget amounts for next month.

Expenses/Bills	Income/Extras
Mortgage _____	Income from Work: _____
Utilities _____	
Transportation _____	Other Income (List):
Household Expenses _____	_____ _____
Dinning _____	_____ _____
Entertainment _____	_____ _____
Health Insurance _____	_____ _____
Kids _____	Savings:
Giving _____	_____ _____
Miscellaneous _____	
Total Expenses:	**Total Income:**

MONTH 9

Prosperity Focus

For I have plans for you

"Declares the Lord"

Plans to Prosper you

and not harm you

Plans to give you a hope &
a future

Jer. 29:11

Monthly *Income*

Date Received	Income Amount
Monthly Total:	

Monthly Utilities *Expense*

Date	Description	Amount	Balance

Monthly Transportation *Expense*

Date	Description	Amount	Balance

Monthly Household *Expense*

Date	Description	Amount	Balance

Monthly Giving

Date	Description	Amount	Balance

Monthly Dinning *Expense*

Date	Description	Amount	Balance

Monthly Entertainment *Expense*

Date	Description	Amount	Balance

Monthly Kids *Expense*

Date	Description	Amount	Balance

Monthly Miscellaneous *Expense*

Date	Description	Amount	Balance

Monthly SAVINGS

Date	Amount Saved	Balance

Debt Plan

Date	Description	Amount	Balance

MONTH AT A GLANCE

The Month Of : _____

Starting Bal: [   ]

Expenses/Bills

Mortgage _____

Utilities _____

Transportation _____

Household Expenses _____

Dinning _____

Entertainment _____

Health Insurance _____

Kids _____

Giving _____

Miscellaneous _____

Total Expenses:

Income/Extras

Income from Work : _____

Other Income (List):

_____   _____

_____   _____

_____   _____

_____   _____

Savings:

_____   _____

Total Income:

Ending Balance:

Month End Reflection:

1. Take a look at your Monthly expenses detail sheets. List in order (from most expensive to least expensive) your expenses.

_____
_____
_____
_____
_____
_____
_____
_____
_____
_____

2. Take a look at your Monthly expenses detail Sheets. In what areas can you reduce your spending?

_____
_____
_____
_____
_____
_____
_____
_____
_____

3. Is there additional funds that you can put in your savings account? If so how much? How much are you willing to put in your savings Next Month?

_____
_____
_____
_____
_____

4. Are there any funds that can be directed towards your debt? If so how much can you add to a monthly bill next month?

_____
_____
_____
_____
_____

5. **Monthly Goals:** Using the information from your reflection along with your Month at a glance sheet fill in your goals/estimated budget amounts for next month.

Expenses/Bills	Income/Extras
Mortgage _____	Income from Work: _____
Utilities _____	
Transportation _____	Other Income (List):
Household Expenses _____	_____ _____
Dinning _____	_____ _____
Entertainment _____	_____ _____
Health Insurance _____	Savings:
Kids _____	_____ _____
Miscellaneous _____	
Total Expenses:	**Total Income:**

MONTH 10

Prosperity Focus

POOR
IS HE WHO WORKS WITH

A NEGLIGENT HAND

BUT THE HAND OF THE DILIGENT

MAKES RICH

PROVERBS 10:4

Monthly *Income*

Date Received	Income Amount
Monthly Total:	

Monthly Utilities *Expense*

Date	Description	Amount	Balance

Monthly Transportation *Expense*

Date	Description	Amount	Balance

Monthly Household *Expense*

Date	Description	Amount	Balance

Monthly Giving

Date	Description	Amount	Balance

Monthly Dinning *Expense*

Date	Description	Amount	Balance

Monthly Entertainment *Expense*

Date	Description	Amount	Balance

Monthly Kids *Expense*

Date	Description	Amount	Balance

Monthly Miscellaneous *Expense*

Date	Description	Amount	Balance

Monthly *SAVINGS*

Date	Amount Saved	Balance

Debt Plan

Date	Description	Amount	Balance

MONTH AT A GLANCE

The Month Of : _____

Starting Bal: [   ]

Expenses/Bills | Income/Extras

Mortgage _____

Utilities _____

Transportation _____

Household Expenses _____

Dinning _____

Entertainment _____

Health Insurance _____

Kids _____

Giving _____

Miscellaneous _____

Total Expenses:

Income from Work : _____

Other Income (List):

_____ _____

_____ _____

_____ _____

_____ _____

Savings:

_____ _____

Total Income:

Ending Balance:

Month End Reflection:

1. Take a look at your Monthly expenses detail sheets. List in order (from most expensive to least expensive) your expenses.

_____
_____
_____
_____
_____
_____
_____
_____

2. Take a look at your Monthly expenses detail Sheets. In what areas can you reduce your spending?

_____
_____
_____
_____
_____
_____
_____
_____

3. Is there additional funds that you can put in your savings account? If so how much? How much are you willing to put in your savings Next Month?

_____
_____
_____
_____
_____

4. Are there any funds that can be directed towards your debt? If so how much can you add to a monthly bill next month?

_____
_____
_____
_____
_____

5. **Monthly Goals:** Using the information from your reflection along with your Month at a glance sheet fill in your goals/estimated budget amounts for next month.

Expenses/Bills	Income/Extras
Mortgage _____	Income from Work: _____
Utilities _____	
Transportation _____	Other Income (List):
Household Expenses _____	_____ _____
Dinning _____	_____ _____
Entertainment _____	_____ _____
Health Insurance _____	_____ _____
Kids _____	Savings: _____ _____
Giving _____	
Miscellaneous _____	
Total Expenses:	**Total Income:**

MONTH 11

Prosperity Focus

Remember this:

The work I am putting in now

Is For

My Legacy!

I will stay focused on the budget I have put in place so that my legacy learns how to be good stewards and can be blessed by what I have stored up for them.

Amanda Latrice

Monthly *Income*

Date Received	Income Amount
Monthly Total:	

Monthly Utilities *Expense*

Date	Description	Amount	Balance

Monthly Transportation *Expense*

Date	Description	Amount	Balance

Monthly Household *Expense*

Date	Description	Amount	Balance

Monthly Giving

Date	Description	Amount	Balance

Monthly Dinning *Expense*

Date	Description	Amount	Balance

Monthly Entertainment *Expense*

Date	Description	Amount	Balance

Monthly Kids *Expense*

Date	Description	Amount	Balance

Monthly Miscellaneous *Expense*

Date	Description	Amount	Balance

Monthly SAVINGS

Date	Amount Saved	Balance

Debt Plan

Date	Description	Amount	Balance

MONTH AT A GLANCE

The Month Of: _____

Starting Bal: [   ]

Expenses/Bills | Income/Extras

Mortgage _____

Utilities _____

Transportation _____

Household Expenses _____

Dinning _____

Entertainment _____

Health Insurance _____

Kids _____

Giving _____

Miscellaneous _____

Total Expenses:

Income from Work: _____

Other Income (List):

_____ _____

_____ _____

_____ _____

_____ _____

Savings:

_____ _____

Total Income:

Ending Balance:

Month End Reflection:

1. Take a look at your Monthly expenses detail sheets. List in order (from most expensive to least expensive) your expenses.

_____

_____

_____

_____

_____

_____

_____

_____

_____

2. Take a look at your Monthly expenses detail Sheets. In what areas can you reduce your spending?

_____

_____

_____

_____

_____

_____

_____

_____

_____

3. Is there additional funds that you can put in your savings account? If so how much? How much are you willing to put in your savings Next Month?

_____
_____
_____
_____
_____

4. Are there any funds that can be directed towards your debt? If so how much can you add to a monthly bill next month?

_____
_____
_____
_____
_____

5. **Monthly Goals:** Using the information from your reflection along with your Month at a glance sheet fill in your goals/estimated budget amounts for next month.

Expenses/Bills	Income/Extras
Mortgage _____	Income from Work: _____
Utilities _____	
Transportation _____	Other Income (List):
Household Expenses _____	_____ _____
Dinning _____	_____ _____
Entertainment _____	_____ _____
Health Insurance _____	_____ _____
Kids _____	Savings: _____ _____
Giving _____	
Miscellaneous _____	**Total Income:**
Total Expenses:	

MONTH 12

New Business Owner's Declaration

(By Amanda Latrice)

I declare that I have been called and chosen by God for such a time as this to write the vision and make it plain in the earth.

I declare the strategies to maintain proper clientele in every demographic that God has called me to is being downloaded to me in the name of Jesus.

I declare that because God has chosen me HE is opening up opportunities and the resources to produce HIS vision for this business.

I declare that throughout this journey God will provide me with mentors that will help guide me and provide the feedback needed for my growth spiritually and naturally in every area.

I declare that I will have God's love for all of my clients, customers, employees, and partners because HE has sent them.

I declare that the business environment has been cultivated in HIS presence and it is a safe place for clients and employees.

I declare that I will be a boss that not only teaches but remains teachable.

I declare that I will be a boss that is concerned with the development of the whole person, so that employees grow into their destinies, identities, and callings.

I declare that even as HE makes this business expand and become successful that I will not fall into the traps of pride, greed, or idolatry. This business belongs to HIM and every part of the finances and its success is for HIS glory.

Just as HE has called and chosen me, HE has done the same for many in the body of Christ. I declare that I will encourage and support them in whatever way the Lord may ask of me. I declare that the spirit of competition has no right in the Kingdom of God and I will not take part in it.

Perfect love cast out all fear, so I declare that because of God's perfect love for me, all insecurities and fears of this journey into the business world are being cast out and ground into dust in the name Jesus.

I declare that only God's truth will stand, and it is only HIS truth that is taking root in my inward parts and developing my identity.
I declare that I am mounting up in God's strength and endurance so that I can work on each step of the strategy in HIS timing and not become worn down by the process.

I declare that even during the trying times in this journey God is filling me with HIS overflowing joy, and I will stay in a place of peace because this is part of my destiny alignment.

I declare with confidence THIS DAY that I am shifting into the fullness of having a Business mindset with a Kingdom Perspective, and I will not water down or devalue the vision that you have granted to my hands, but I will produce it in the excellence of HIS name.

It is so and established. IN JESUS Name, Amen!

Monthly *Income*

Date Received	Income Amount
Monthly Total:	

Monthly Utilities *Expense*

Date	Description	Amount	Balance

Monthly Transportation *Expense*

Date	Description	Amount	Balance

Monthly Household *Expense*

Date	Description	Amount	Balance

Monthly Giving

Date	Description	Amount	Balance

Monthly Dinning *Expense*

Date	Description	Amount	Balance

Monthly Entertainment *Expense*

Date	Description	Amount	Balance

Monthly Kids *Expense*

Date	Description	Amount	Balance

Monthly Miscellaneous *Expense*

Date	Description	Amount	Balance

Monthly *SAVINGS*

Date	Amount Saved	Balance

Debt Plan

Date	Description	Amount	Balance

MONTH AT A GLANCE

The Month Of: _____

Starting Bal: _____

Expenses/Bills	Income/Extras
Mortgage _____	Income from Work: _____
Utilities _____	
Transportation _____	Other Income (List):
Household Expenses _____	_____ _____
Dinning _____	_____ _____
Entertainment _____	_____ _____
Health Insurance _____	_____ _____
Kids _____	Savings:
Giving _____	_____ _____
Miscellaneous _____	
Total Expenses:	**Total Income:**

Ending Balance:

Month End Reflection:

1. Take a look at your Monthly expenses detail sheets. List in order (from most expensive to least expensive) your expenses.

_____
_____
_____
_____
_____
_____
_____
_____
_____

2. Take a look at your Monthly expenses detail Sheets. In what areas can you reduce your spending?

_____
_____
_____
_____
_____
_____
_____
_____

3. Is there additional funds that you can put in your savings account? If so how much? How much are you willing to put in your savings Next Month?

_____
_____
_____
_____
_____

4. Are there any funds that can be directed towards your debt? If so how much can you add to a monthly bill next month?

_____
_____
_____
_____
_____

5. **Monthly Goals:** Using the information from your reflection along with your Month at a glance sheet fill in your goals/estimated budget amounts for next month.

Expenses/Bills	Income/Extras
Mortgage _____	Income from Work: _____
Utilities _____	
Transportation _____	Other Income (List):
Household Expenses _____	_____ _____
Dinning _____	_____ _____
Entertainment _____	_____ _____
Health Insurance _____	_____ _____
Kids _____	Savings: _____ _____
Giving _____	
Miscellaneous _____	**Total Income:**
Total Expenses:	

Year End Reflection

Take time to reflect on the 12 months that you have been budgeting and set goals for what you will do in the next 12 months.

1. What changes did you make during the year that you feel are beneficial to take into the next 12 months?

2. What are some goals for your finances that you would like to implement in your budget for the next 12 months?

3. What areas do you feel you could have done better and would like to do better in the next 12 months?

4. What are your desires concerning your finances? Write a declaration that you can utilize throughout the 12 months.

Sowing in the Press

In Jewish culture oil was a commodity because there was so many ways to use it. It was used for lighting, cooking, beautifications processes, anointing of kings, a cancelation of debt and a sustaining of provision. It was considered a sign of prosperity and stability. In 2kings 4:1-7 we find a widowed woman carrying the burden of her husband's debts. Because she did not have the money to pay the creditors, the creditors were requiring her sons to work for them to pay off the debts. She reached out to Elisha who knew her husband and his question to her was "What do you have in the house?" She told Elisha I have nothing just a pot of oil. As the widow adhered to Elisha's instructions the oil she had was what she needed to cancel her debts and provide for her household beyond paying for the debt.

2 Kings 4 Expanded Bible (EXB)
The wife of a man from the ·groups [company; brotherhood; ᴸ sons] of prophets said to Elisha, "Your servant, my husband, is dead. You know he ·honored [revered; feared] the LORD. But now ·the man he owes money to [a creditor] is coming to take my two boys as his slaves!"

Elisha answered, "How can I help you? Tell me, what do you have in your house?"
The woman said, "I don't have anything there except a ·pot [jar; flask]of oil."

Then Elisha said, "Go and get empty jars from all your neighbors. Don't ask for just a few.

Then go into your house and shut the door behind you and your sons. Pour oil into all the jars and set the full ones aside."

So she left Elisha and shut the door behind her and her sons. As they brought the jars to her, she poured out the oil.

When the jars were all full, she said to her son, "Bring me another jar." But he said, "There are no more jars." Then the oil stopped flowing.

She went and told Elisha. And the prophet said to her, "Go, sell the oil and pay ·what you owe [your debts]. You and your sons can live on what is left."

In a season where we feel like multiple areas of our lives are burdensome we may respond just like the widowed women. In those moments we may feel financially, emotionally, professionally, personally, mentally drained, and like we need to be poured into or blessed and God has the nerve to say what do you have in your house…..Really God? As I was looking at the scripture and thinking about that, I know my response has been "I have nothing to give." "In the midst of financial hardship are you really asking me what is in my house to give?" Unlike my response, the widowed women did not stop there she said I have this pot of oil. To the widowed women that did not mean much. If she used it for light it would be gone soon and that did not really help the family, so what good was it? In the midst of one of hardest challenges of her life she was willing to give whatever to keep her family. What she did not realize was that her willingness to give the pot of oil was her power to get wealth being activated (Deuteronomy 8:18).

In the midst of financial hardships, it is easy to stop sowing and tell God I have nothing to give, but there is something in us that God is requiring us to sow. When we sow under his instruction we tap into the miracle power of God that allows the wells of prosperity and stability to open up on our behalf. Elisha gave the widowed women instructions to gather vases and then close herself and her sons in the house and fill them all. The miraculous power of God was able to operate in her giving what she had. Even though she did not understand at the beginning she trusted the wisdom and words of Elisha and the obedience and alignment allowed the oil to flow until all of her vases were filled.

It is never that God is not mindful of what is going on in our lives even though it feels like it. God is requiring a shift in us and a level of yielding our control. Our finances are not our own so God will require us to give in the press so that we posture ourselves in a place that allows him to have full control thus allowing miracles, abundance, blessings, and freedom to flow in our lives.

Financial Prayer

(By: Amanda Latrice)

Financial provision is our portion! We declare we are being over taken by the blessings of God in our household. No lack will operate in our home and in our finances in the name of Jesus. We overthrow every siege set up against the provision and blessings for our household and finances right now in the name of Jesus. We close, lock, and apply the blood and fire of Jesus to every door that would try to bring financial famine, dishonor, demotion, cycling, stagnation, and limited progress. We declare that the full benefits of God are our portion. We cleanse and gut out any blockages in our spirit and soul that would hinder us from receiving your correction, guidance, direction, and truth for our finances father. We break all powers of weariness, oppression, and depression, that may have entered from the burden of life situations right now in the name of Jesus.

We repent for any way we have mishandled our finances father. We cleanse and gut out all fear of that has opened us up to lack or greed father. We burn it out by fire right now in the name of Jesus. We call forth healing to the places that have been wounded in the past that have caused us to control our finances in a way that does not exalt you or put you first. We repent and ask you to cleanse out any way we have operated in the victim mentality as a means to justify how we have handled our finances. Gut out and burn by fire every place in the personality and identity that has accepted or enmeshed with lack and poverty right name of Jesus. We declare today to Hell ENOUGH IS ENOUGH over our finances. We mount up in our God given authority as kingdom heirs and declare:

- That every seed that we have sown will produce for us a great harvest.
- That blessings will be drawn to us, and overflow and breakthrough in our finances is our portion (Luke 6:38).
- That we will not lack because God is causing us to prosper in this season (Ps 35:27)
- That our soul, health, and all that concerns us is prospering as he releases his renewed mind upon us (3 John 1:2).
- That we abide in him and in him we find all things. We choose today to walk in abundance (Philippians 4:9, 2 Corinthians 9:8).
- That we shift to being properly positioned by the rivers of living water where we will bring forth fruit and all that we put our hands to is blessed and will prosper (Ps 1:3)
- That wealth and riches will be in our house and righteousness endures forever (Ps 112:2).
- That I HAVE THE POWER TO CREATE WEALTH! I will tap into not only the power but the wisdom and guidance of the Lord to produce and reproduce in this season.

We seal ourselves in that and decree breakthrough is our portion and we command fruit to follow.

In Jesus Name, Amen

References

Adobe Spark . (n.d.). Retrieved September 2018, from https://www.spark.adobe.com/

Canva. (n.d.). Retrieved September 2018, from https://www.canva.com/

Dictionary.com. (n.d.). Retrieved June 10, 2017, from http://www.dictionary.com/

Strong, J. (1890). *Strong's exhaustive concordance of the Bible.* **Abingdon Press**

BibleGateway. (n.d.). Retrieved June 10, 2017, from https://www.biblegateway.com/

Book Cover by Expressive Expressions by T. Nicole
Connect with her on Facebook

Back cover picture from freepik.com

www.ingramcontent.com/pod-product-compliance
Lightning Source LLC
Chambersburg PA
CBHW080604080426
42453CB00031B/2275